For Etta

Orchard Books, A division of Franklin Watts, Inc.
387 Park Avenue South, New York, NY 10016

Manufactured in the United States of America
Produced in Great Britain by Mathew Price Ltd
Printed by General Offset Co., Inc.
Bound by Horowitz/Rae. Book design by Mina Greenstein
The text of this book is set in 20 pt. ITC Century Book.
The illustrations are pen and ink and watercolors, reproduced in full color.
10 9 8 7 6 5 4 3 2 1

Library of Congress Cataloging-in-Publication Data
Stickland, Paul. A child's book of things / by Paul Stickland.—1st American ed.
p. cm. Summary: Labeled illustrations of common objects are accompanied
by an illustration depicting all the objects in place.
ISBN 0-531-05906-5. ISBN 0-531-08506-6 (lib. bdg.)
1. Vocabulary—juvenile literature. [1. Vocabulary.] I. Title.
PE1449.S77 1990   428.1—dc20   90-30647 CIP AC

A Child's Book of THINGS

PAUL STICKLAND

Orchard Books   New York

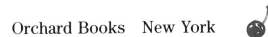

book

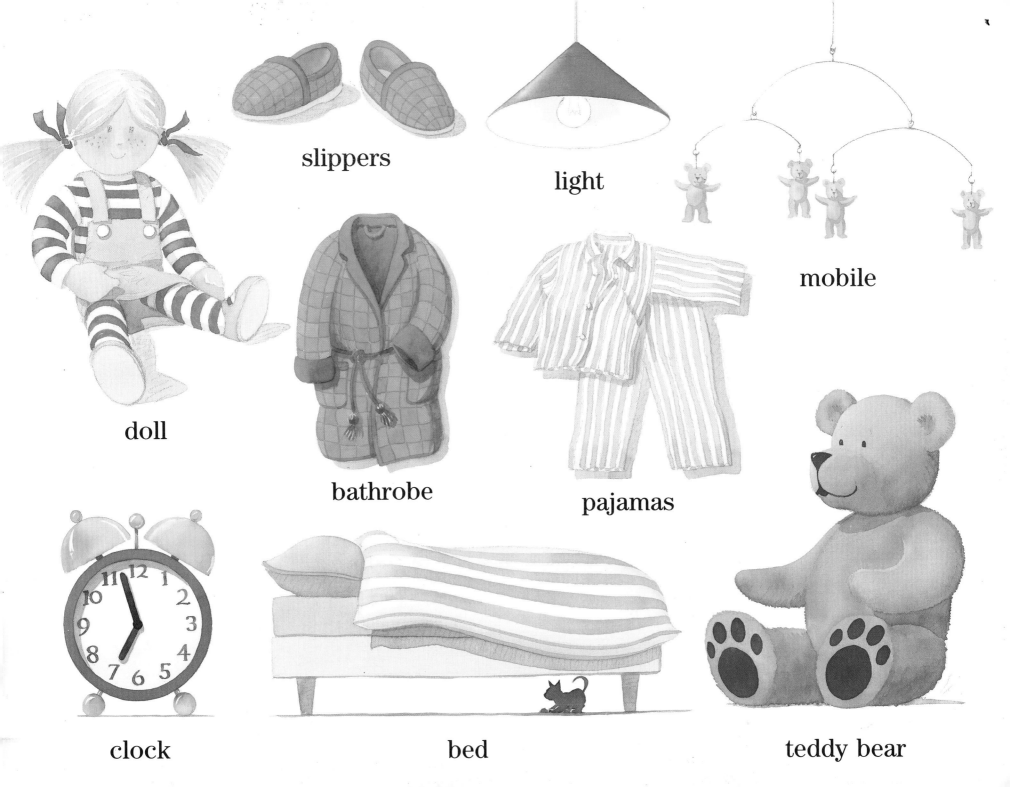

slippers

light

mobile

doll

bathrobe

pajamas

clock

bed

teddy bear

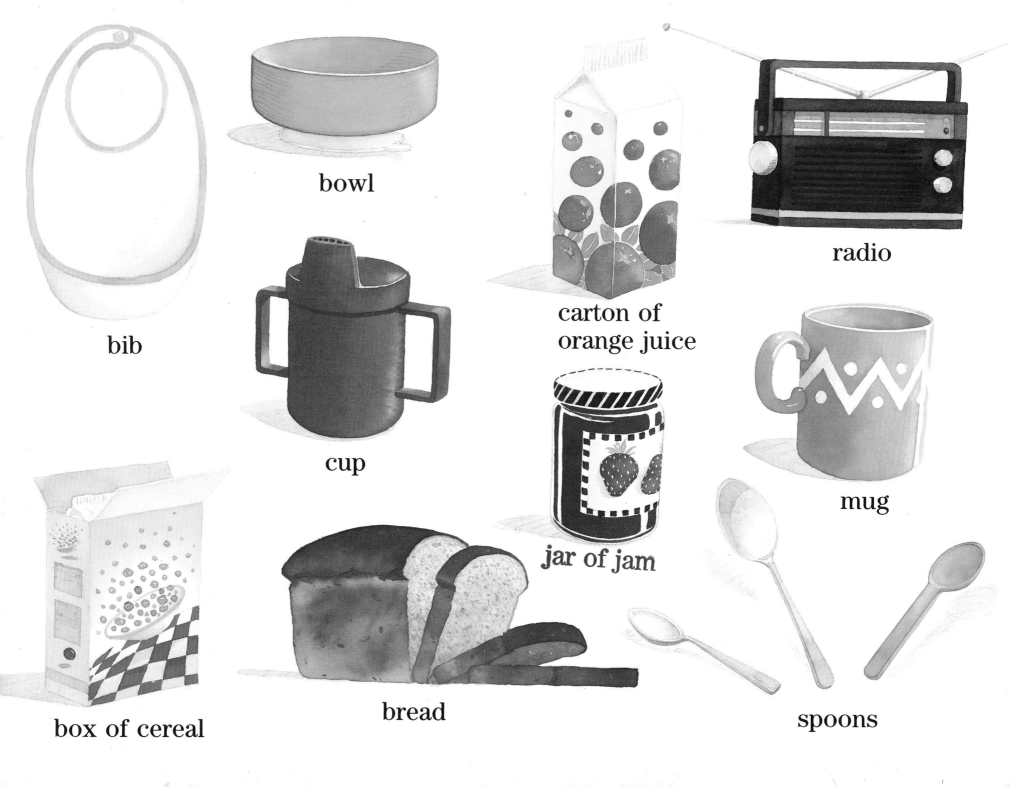

bib

bowl

cup

carton of
orange juice

jar of jam

radio

mug

box of cereal

bread

spoons

egg

carton of milk

eggcup

cat's bowl

sweater

socks

overalls

shirt

dress

pants

skirt

laundry basket

tights

underpants

T-shirt

tank top

sleeper

box of
laundry soap

washing machine

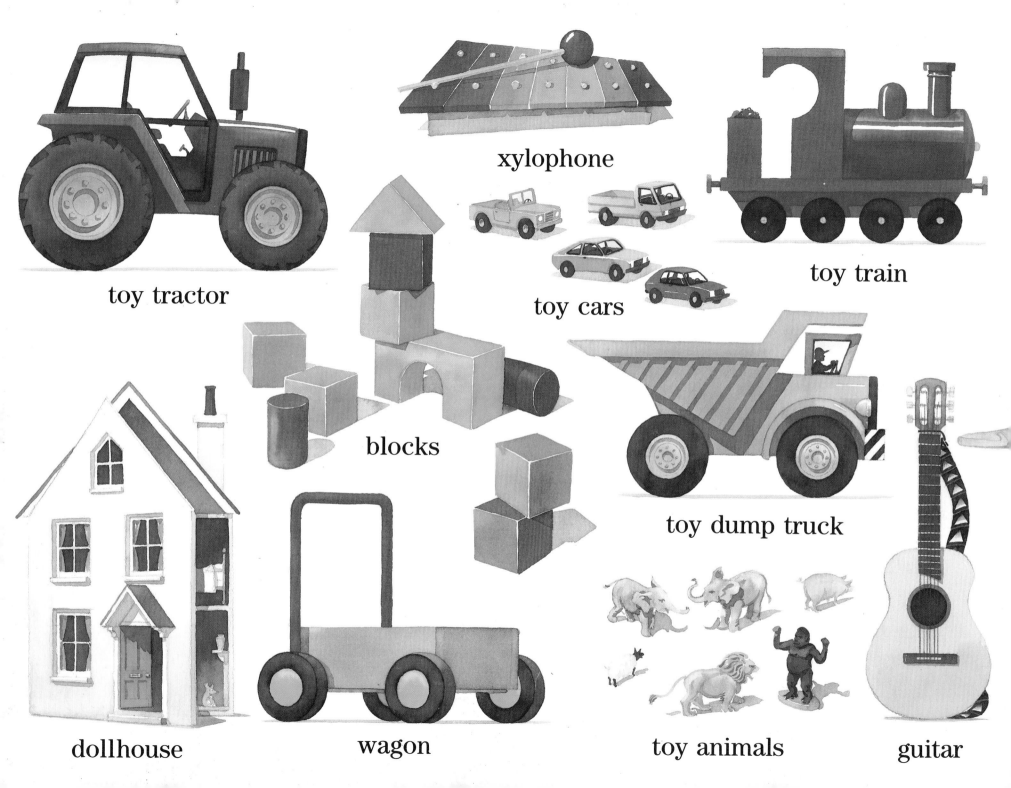

toy tractor

xylophone

toy train

toy cars

blocks

toy dump truck

dollhouse

wagon

toy animals

guitar

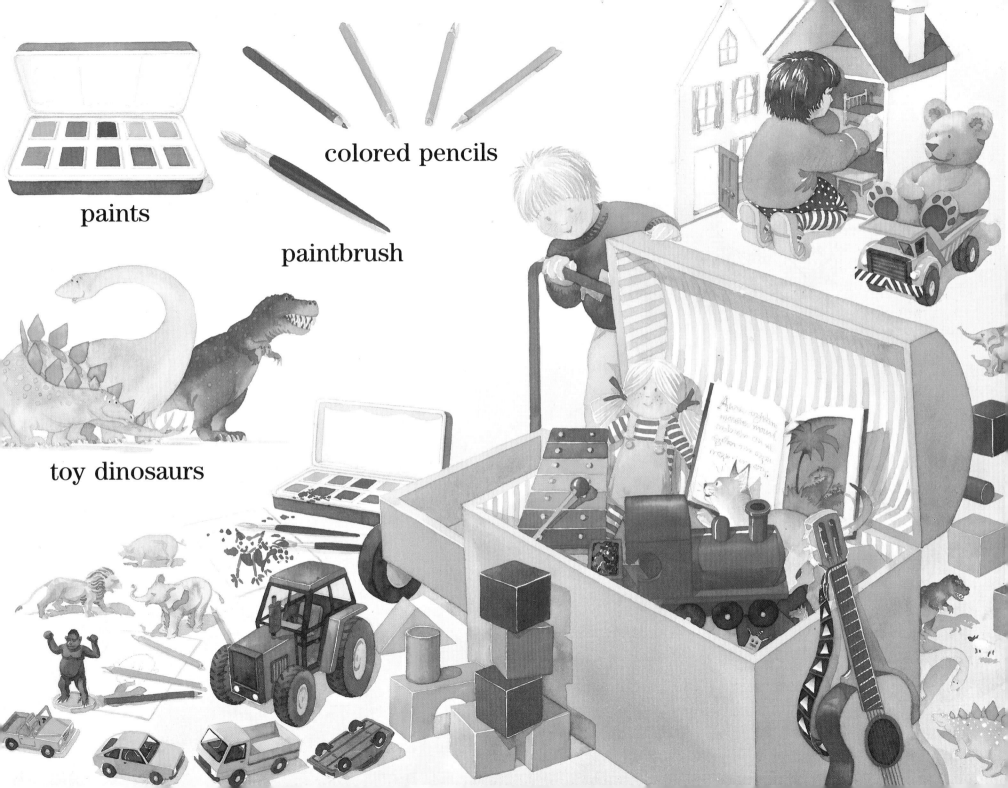

paints

colored pencils

paintbrush

toy dinosaurs

keys

hook

doorknob

keyhole

letters

doormat

shoes

hat

coat

umbrella

boots

gloves

scarf

basket

stroller

bicycle

apple

banana

cherries

strawberries

lemon

orange

melon

plum

lettuce

tomato

peas

corn on the cob

cans

package of
cookies

potato

beans

onion

grapes

pear

jar of honey

container of
yogurt

raspberries

carrots

cheese

cup and saucer

colander

plate

kettle

lid

pitcher

saucepan

frying pan

bottle of
dishwashing liquid

wooden
spoon

teapot

garbage pail

cardboard box

vacuum cleaner

sponge mop

ironing board

can of polish

broom

dustpan

brush

rag

iron

feather
duster

leaf

wheelbarrow

beetle

bird

butterfly

trowel

fork

lawn mower

plant

rake

shovel

watering can

flowerpots

seed tray

ladybug

worm

saw

nuts and
bolts

screws

screwdriver   pliers   vise grip

wood   ladder   toolbox   hammer

nails

vise

spider

paintbrush

can of oil

can of
paint

mirror

antenna

window handle

steering wheel

wrenches

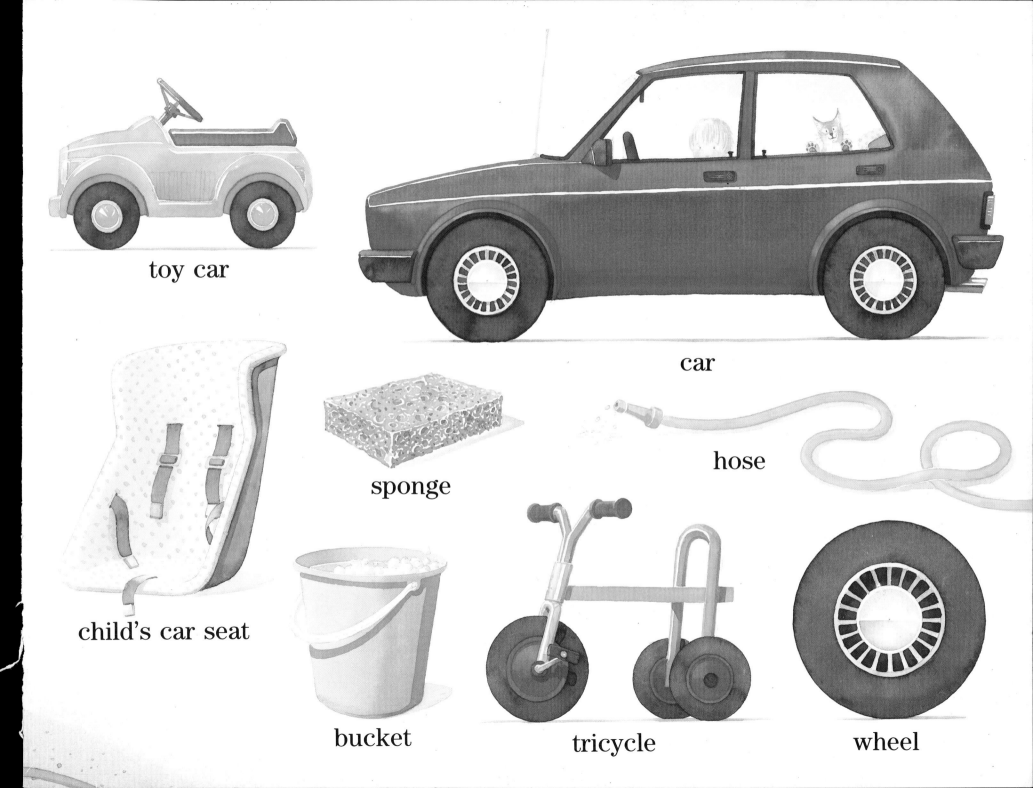

toy car

car

child's car seat

sponge

hose

bucket

tricycle

wheel

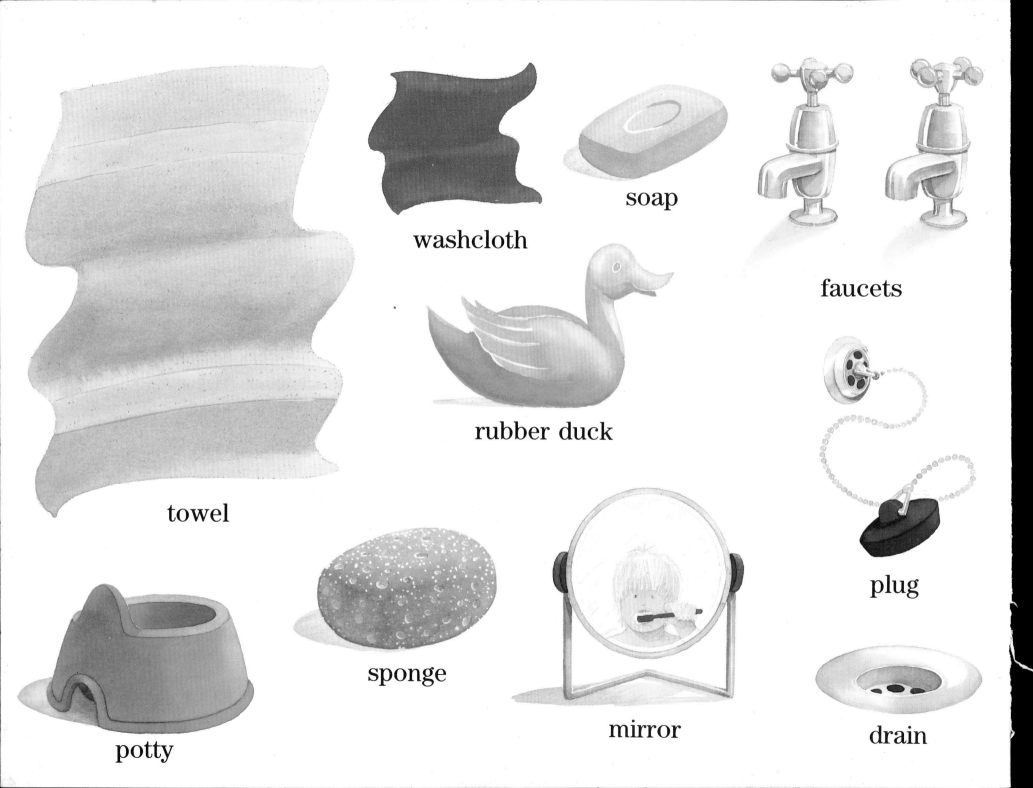

washcloth

soap

faucets

rubber duck

plug

towel

potty

sponge

mirror

drain

toothbrush

toothpaste